When I **Grow Up...**

Firefighter

Written by Clare Hibbert
Illustrated by Mike Byrne

Bromley Libraries

Consultant: Dean Fenton
of the London Fire Brigade

LADYBIRD BOOKS

UK | USA | Canada | Ireland | Australia
India | New Zealand | South Africa

Ladybird Books is part of the Penguin Random House group of companies
whose addresses can be found at global.penguinrandomhouse.com.

ladybird.com

Penguin
Random House
UK

First published 2015
001

Copyright © Ladybird Books Ltd, 2015

Ladybird and the Ladybird logo are registered trademarks owned by Ladybird Books Ltd

The moral right of the author and illustrator has been asserted

Printed in China

A CIP catalogue record for this book is available from the British Library

ISBN: 978–0–723–29470–2

Contents

What do firefighters do? 4

The fire station 6

Daily life 8

Dressed for work 10

Inside the fire engine 12

Tools for the job 14

Fire vehicles 16

Fire! Fire! 18

Rescue 20

Working together 22

Disasters 24

Being a good firefighter 26

Keeping homes safe 28

Being prepared 30

Glossary 32

What do firefighters do?

Being a firefighter is a very important job. Firefighters save lives and buildings. Look at some of the things that they do each day.

Putting out fires

Giving advice about how to avoid fires

Rescuing people

Helping at car crashes

Working hard at any time of the day or night

The fire station

The fire station is the firefighters' base. They can be called out to emergencies from here. Fire engines and equipment are kept here, too.

Most of the fire station is a big garage space.

If the alarm sounds, the crew must be ready to act.

The duty officer learns about an emergency from control. He passes the information on to the crew.

Daily life

When they are not out at emergencies, firefighters carry out drills. They practise the important skills they will need in a fire.

The firefighters use a dummy to practise carrying people to safety.

The firefighters practise rolling out their hoses on the ground.

Firefighters work different shifts. That means they sometimes have to get up at strange times.

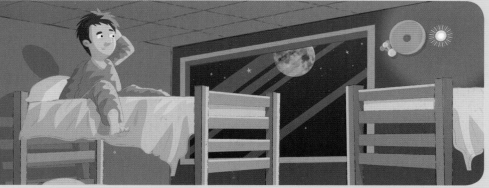

The firefighters use a ladder to practise rescues from windows.

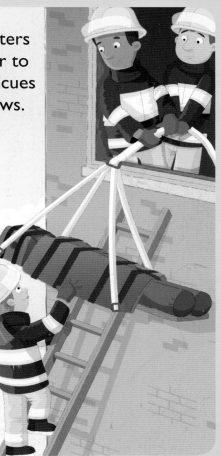

The firefighters check the fire engine has all the right equipment on board.

9

Dressed for work

Firefighters wear a uniform to protect them at work. It makes them stand out so people know they are there to help in an emergency.

helmet

visor

breathing equipment

tunic

walkie-talkie

torch

The helmet and visor protect the firefighter's head and face.

Firefighters have breathing equipment to help them breathe inside a smoky building.

They carry a torch so they can see in dark spaces.

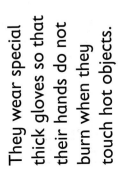

trousers

steel-toed boots

reflective strip

gloves

They wear special thick gloves so that their hands do not burn when they touch hot objects.

Their tunic and trousers are made of special material that won't catch fire. They are waterproof, too.

The clothes have reflective strips that shine when light falls on them. They make the uniform easier to see in the dark.

11

Inside the fire engine

The front of the fire engine is where the firefighters sit. The back has handy compartments for storing equipment.

siren

ladder

MDT screen

Mobile data terminal (MDT) showing where the emergency is

Oxygen tank and mask

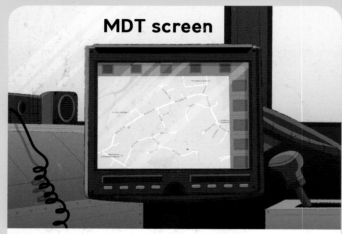

Tools inside compartments

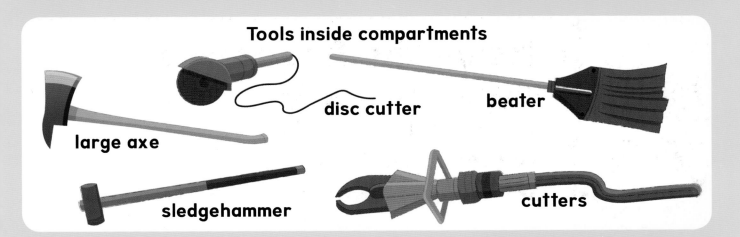

large axe

disc cutter

beater

sledgehammer

cutters

Water foam pump bay

Reels and hoses

13

Tools for the job

Firefighters need lots of different equipment and tools. These things help to keep the firefighters safe in dangerous situations.

Breathing equipment

Firefighters wear oxygen masks so they can breathe in very smoky conditions. The entry control officer uses a board to show how much oxygen is left in each of the firefighters' tanks.

Entry control board

Protective suit

Firefighters have special suits to protect them when they are working with dangerous chemicals.

Thermal imaging camera

Firefighters have cameras that allow them to see areas of heat so they can find people quickly.

Sandbags

Firefighters use sandbags during floods. These soak up water and stop it getting into buildings.

Cutters

Firefighters can use cutters for breaking locks when they need to get in somewhere quickly.

Fire vehicles

Fire engines carry firefighters to emergencies at top speed. There are other vehicles for areas that cannot be reached by road.

There might be two or three fire engines racing to an emergency at one time! Their sirens warn other road users to get out of the way.

Firefighting tanks have tracks so they can travel easily over rough ground.

Firefighting planes can put out fires from the air when it is too dangerous down on the ground.

When fire boats fight fires, they can pump water straight from the sea or the river.

Firefighting trains put out fires on trains, railway tracks and in tunnels.

Fire! Fire!

There's been a call to the station. A house is on fire. Firefighters leap on board the fire engine. They zoom to the rescue, sirens blaring.

When they arrive, the firefighters connect their hoses to a water hydrant in the ground.

Now they work really hard spraying the flames with water.

They have put out the fire. It will be months before the house is fit to live in again, but thankfully, everyone is safe.

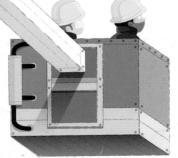

Rescue

Fires happen in all sorts of places, from shops to airports. Firefighters know how to rescue people from lots of different situations.

Inside buildings

Firefighters use torches to see in the darkness. They have walkie-talkies to stay in touch.

High-rise rescues

This super-tall ladder is called an aerial platform ladder. It lifts the firefighters very high and has hoses fixed to it for fighting the fire.

Airport fires

Very big airports have their own fire stations. If a plane catches fire, the firefighters are there right away.

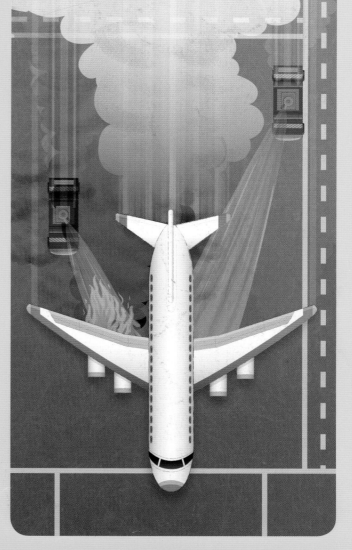

Working together

Firefighters often work alongside police, paramedics or other emergency services. Together they make sure the public are safe.

At this car crash, the police officer is making sure people stay safely behind the line.

The firefighters use their cutters to get into the car and rescue the people inside. They can give first aid, too.

When the paramedics arrive they give more medical help. They take badly injured people to hospital.

Disasters

Many different disasters happen around the world. Some damage the environment. Firefighters are always there to help.

Oil spills

If oil leaks from a ship, it can catch fire or poison sea life. Firefighters work to stop this happening.

Mining rescues

Using explosives in mines can cause accidents. Firefighters can rescue miners from deep underground.

Forest fires

In some places, forest fires may happen in the hot summer months. Sometimes a flash of lightning starts the fire. The flames spread quickly through the dry wood and leaves.

Earthquakes

Some parts of the world have big earthquakes, when the ground shakes and pulls apart. Roads and buildings are destroyed and this can start fires or cause floods.

Being a good firefighter

Firefighters have to be amazingly brave.
Day or night, they risk their lives in dangerous
situations to rescue complete strangers.

Firefighters need to be strong and fit.
Sometimes they have to climb a lot
of stairs and carry heavy equipment.

Firefighters need to be fearless.
It takes great courage to run
into a burning building!

Firefighters have to work in extreme conditions. Even in the freezing cold they still fight fires. No wonder people think of them as real-life superheroes!

Firefighters work with lots of different people.

They need to help them to stay safe and calm.

Keeping homes safe

Firefighters advise people how to prevent fires. They give lots of helpful tips on how to keep people's homes safe.

ALWAYS remember to check if your smoke alarm is working.

A working smoke alarm detects smoke to tell you there's a fire.

DON'T put clothes or anything else on top of lamps.

Clothes should be put away. They can catch fire on a lamp.

ALWAYS have an adult in the kitchen with you when something is cooking.

It is dangerous to be alone near a hot hob or oven.

NEVER put water near electrical equipment.

Wet wires and sockets can start a fire.

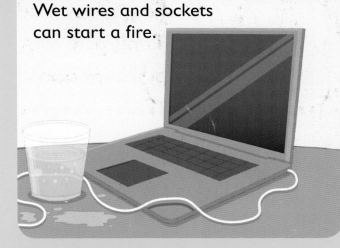

ALWAYS keep fires in your fireplace safe with a fireguard.

Tell a grown-up if there isn't a fireguard in place.

NEVER play with matches.

Tell a grown-up if you see any matches that haven't been put away safely.

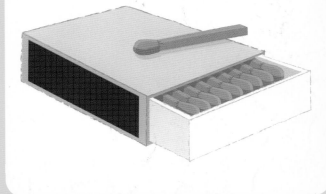

Being prepared

Firefighters visit schools to tell teachers and children how to stay safe in a fire. It is important to practise fire drills, too.

1 When the fire alarm goes off, everyone must leave their belongings behind and walk quickly and calmly out of the building.

2 The teacher takes a register to make sure everybody is there.

3 The teachers check how quickly everyone got out. Practising fire drills means everyone will know what to do if there is a real fire.

Glossary

base
The place where firefighters start out from and where they return to.

control
Short for the control centre – the place that receives emergency calls for the fire service.

drill
An exercise that people do to practise how they will act in a situation.

dummy
A pretend body that firefighters can use for practice rescues.

emergency
A dangerous or serious situation such as a fire or a car crash.

entry control officer
An officer who checks that the firefighters have enough oxygen in their tanks with an entry control board during an emergency.

fire brigade
An organization that works to fight fires.

paramedic
An ambulance worker trained to give emergency first aid as a patient is rushed to hospital.

shift
The period of time (usually around eight hours) that someone is at work. At the fire station, shifts are planned so that there are firefighters working at all times.

smoke alarm
A device that can tell if there is smoke in the air. When it detects smoke, it flashes and makes a warning noise.